bOn jOvi

BILL BATEMAN

ORION

AN ORION PAPERBACK

This is a Carlton Book

First published in Great Britain in 1994 by Orion Books Ltd, Orion House, 5 Upper St Martin's Lane, London, WC2H 9EA.

A CIP catalogue record for this book is available from the British Library.

ISBN 1 85797 327 5

Edited, designed and typeset by Impact Editions
Printed in Italy

THE AUTHOR

One of the UK's foremost rock journalists, Bill Bateman is well known for his work in many of the music world's leading periodicals. An early job as a unicyclist prepared him for the pressure of writing at the highest level. He lives at home in comfort with his pet python Simon.

CONTENTS

INTRODUCTION..6

CHAPTER 1: THE EARLY YEARS.............................10

CHAPTER 2: GETTING HOTTER 26

CHAPTER 3: THE SLIPPERY ROAD TO SUPERSTARDOM ...36

CHAPTER 4: THE SYNDICATE..................................44

CHAPTER 5: ALONE & WITH FRIENDS 66

CHAPTER 6: REPAYING THE FAITHFUL.......................96

DISCOGRAPHY 112

CHRONOLOGY 118

INDEX 119

INTRODUCTION

LAY YOUR HANDS ON ME

The sound of the crowd is phenomenal—a solid wall of aural approval. Seven thousand voices cheer in unison. Seven thousand pairs of hands shoot into the air. Wearing a long, patchwork coat, which billows behind him like a superhero's cape, Jon Bon Jovi spreads his arms wide and makes an entrance a world-champion boxer would be proud of.

Seven thousand pairs of eyes strain for a better look. As drummer Tico Torres beats out a hefty drum-tattoo, Jon walks triumphantly to the edge of the stage, self-assured and totally in control, flicks his hair back out of his eyes and invites the crowd to 'Lay Your Hands On Me'. The roar that goes up is deafening as every fan in the arena moves just a little

Jon Bon Jovi—the master of ceremonies.

bit closer to their idol. It's not for nothing that he wears Superman's "S" logo, tattooed on his left shoulder.

The place is Dublin, the year 1988, the date November 1—the first night of Bon Jovi's mammoth *New Jersey* world tour. But really, it could have been just about anywhere in the world at some time or other in the past ten years. One way or another, every Bon Jovi concert has been a special event.

It's difficult to think of a single performer in rock today who can hold an audience in the palm of his hand as skilfully as Jon Bon Jovi. He's one of the great entertainers—the boy from New Jersey who makes every guy feel like part of the gang and every girl feel, at least for an hour or two, like he could be her man.

Getting straight to business in Dublin, after the anthemic thunder of 'Lay Your Hands On Me', the band slam into 'You Give Love A Bad Name', to further riotous applause. A major international hit and a dynamic hard-rock track, it has the crowd bouncing with euphoric enthusiasm—heading straight from that into 'Runaway' is a masterstroke. 'Runaway' is the track that started it all for Bon Jovi, still sounding as fresh, zesty and infectious as ever.

When Jon finally addresses the crowd he tells them he feels like he was born and raised in Dublin—a cliché, for sure, but in the hands of a master showman it induces near-hysteria. He goes

on to ask if anyone wants to join the band and come on the road with him. In an instant he has 7,000 willing volunteers, ready to sign up.

But a great rock 'n' roll band does not live on charisma alone and as they kick off on the 'Homebound Train' there's no ignoring Jon's right-

Hushed anticipation before a Bon Jovi spectacular.

Richie Sambora handin' out hot guitar licks.

hand man, Richie Sambora, knocking out hot 'n' chunky guitar licks Led Zeppelin's Jimmy Page would be proud of. On the organ, David Bryan adds his own solid contribution with some funky keyboard work as the band jam their way round the song's groovy instrumental finale.

Jon pulls a series of party pieces out of the hat. After an adrenalin-pumping 'Wild In The Streets' and an exuberant 'Born To Be My Baby', he asks if they've heard any stories about him being able to fly. If he'd asked about his walking on water, half the audience would probably have roared back in the affirmative. But he settles for flying over the crowd—with the aid of some theatrical apparatus—to play a song from a platform at the other end of the hall.

'I'll Be There For You', a holding-hands, lighters-aloft tearjerker is responsible for a mass outbreak of canoodling by Dublin's young romantics but—by the skin of its teeth—manages to retain a degree of sincerity amidst a flood of sentimentality.

A stream of hits and familiar album tracks follow, climaxing in the energetic highlight of 'Living On A Prayer' and the moody, atmospheric sweep of 'Wanted Dead Or Alive'. But the show's not over yet. Jon has a guest waiting in the wings—Joe Elliott,

Def Leppard frontman, temporary Dublin resident, and, theoretically Jon's biggest rival for the commercial heavy rock crown. Jon loves to jam, and the pair give a rousing rendition of Irish rock legends Thin Lizzy's 'The Boys Are Back In Town', calculated to raise the roof—Jon content to play along on guitar while Elliott handles most of the vocal chores.

In theory it's an untoppable moment, but in practice Jon tops it, finishing off the gig with 'Bad Medicine'—big, bold and brassy, with a cheerfully hammy false ending and a hefty pyrotechnic "oomph" to underline its real finale.

Too good to be true? Never—just another great night for Jon Bon Jovi, the master of ceremonies.

Bon Jovi acknowledge the roaring crowd.

THE EARLY YEARS

The son of John Bongiovi Sr., a hairdresser, and Carol Bongiovi, a former Playboy bunny with unfulfilled acting aspirations, John Francis Bongiovi was born March 2, 1962 and raised in the relatively affluent environment of Sayreville, New Jersey, on the American Eastern Seaboard.

From an early age, he was raised in an atmosphere supportive of his ambitions to make it as a musician—both by virtue of his Jersey surroundings and because his parents were determined that, if John wanted to be a rock star, they'd give him whatever support they could.

"This," said Jon, "is what I'd always wanted since I was in my first band with the kid across the street who played guitar and a drummer who could almost keep a beat and a bass player who had a bass but didn't really know how to play it. But he tried, and we put Beatles tapes on and tried to sing, mimic it.

"It's like anything else…you've got to want it bad enough. If you want it that bad you'll get it."

Like many a would-be rock star with stars in his eyes, he was restless at school (favourite subject: history, but by his own admission "miserable" at English), though attendance at Sayreville High School did give him the opportunity to hook up with David Rashbaum (now better known as Bon Jovi's David Bryan). The two were soon to be found playing R&B

Bon Jovi as you've never seen them before. Left to Right: Tico, Richie, Jon and Dave.

standards in the 10-piece covers-act Atlantic City Expressway.

"We used to play together when we were 16-years-old. We hit the club circuit. We used to go to school and classes would start at 8 in the morning. We'd get there at 8:30, but the teachers would still let us in 'cause they knew we'd been hitting the club scene all night."

BEATEN BY SPRINGSTEEN

While still in his teens, Jon (dropping the "h") graduated to fronting his own act, Jon Bongiovi And The Wild Ones, playing New Jersey clubs like the Fast Lane and opening, at every opportunity, for any of the better-known acts passing through the area.

"Bruce Springsteen was home that summer and the motherfucker would go to the Stone Pony and jam every fuckin' Sunday," he has since recalled. "This was 1982, he had just finished selling out the Garden [New York's Madison Square Garden] ten nights in a row, and he'd be playing a small club every Sunday. Well, my crowd went from 200 to 100 to 23 to 6. Finally we started playing at 8, close the bar at 11, and we'd all go over to the Stone Pony to see Bruce."

Even if Jersey's resident superstar was in the habit of stealing the Wild Ones' Sunday night crowds, Jon

Tico Torres

> **"I PUT THIS BAND TOGETHER AROUND GREAT GUYS RATHER THAN THE GREATEST PLAYERS. I WANTED PEOPLE WHO I COULD GET ALONG WITH, NO EGOS IN THE BAND—EVEN AT CLUB LEVEL."**
>
> *Jon Bon Jovi*

was at least lucky enough to be living in an area with a strong tradition of live rock 'n' roll and a community of musicians contributing to a melting pot of ideas and influences.

"Southside Johnny was on the verge of making it [in 1978]—he was from the backyard. Your choices were to work in the Dupont paint factory or the chemical factory or, like my two best friends, you got out by joining the Navy. Nobody went to university. He made it possible to do the impossible. As a kid, you could go to Asbury Park and see the Dukes [Southside Johnny's band] walking around."

David Bryan

TOO BIG, TOO COOL

There was really no escaping the influence of the Boss—Bruce Springsteen—in whose shadow every Jersey musician walked.

"He was my Beatles, he was like a reality check. When I was 16 I went to see him at the Spectrum in Philadelphia. He opened with 'Badlands', and the whole event was charged with an intensity I'd never witnessed before."

It was, however, lesser-known local musicians from the Jersey scene, rather than Bruce himself, who helped young Jon out—"Bruce Springsteen was too big and too cool to care. He was never nice enough to take our tapes around, he was never a friend of ours."

Instead Jon tips his hat, again, to Southside Johnny, who "did some great things" for him, producing one of his early demos and Lance Larson, who introduced him to Tico Torres. "I remember coming down to this club one night and seeing this wild black drum kit onstage, and I knew I wouldn't like the man playing the drums. Then this wild Cuban came out and banged out a fierce beat and I knew I could never play with anyone else but Tico."

By the Summer of 1982, out of school and dabbling with a variety of part-time work—including

> **"THIS IS WHAT I'D ALWAYS WANTED SINCE I WAS IN MY FIRST BAND WITH THE KID ACROSS THE STREET WHO PLAYED THE GUITAR AND A DRUMMER WHO COULD ALMOST KEEP A BEAT AND A BASS PLAYER WHO HAD A BASS BUT DIDN'T REALLY KNOW HOW TO PLAY IT."**
> *Jon Bon Jovi*

a spell working in a shoe store—Jon had finally landed a job of sorts, sweeping up and carrying out various odd-jobs at the Power Station Studio, a New York recording facility where his cousin, Tony Bongiovi, worked.

The Wild Ones were still wild at heart when they became Bon Jovi.

Alec John Such, who gave Richie a break.

HOME GROWN

Jon followed the time-honoured route of making demos (including one produced by pop-rock solo-artist Billy Squier), and sending them out to every record company he could think of—but failed to make an impact. He had better luck with local radio station WAPT, who liked the track 'Runaway'—a

Richie Sambora—"He had his own style," said Jon.

"SPRINGSTEEN WAS MY BEATLES, HE WAS LIKE A REALITY CHECK. WHEN I WAS 16 I WENT TO SEE HIM AT THE SPECTRUM IN PHILADELPHIA. HE OPENED WITH 'BADLANDS', AND THE WHOLE EVENT WAS CHARGED WITH AN INTENSITY I'D NEVER WITNESSED BEFORE."
Jon Bon Jovi

commercial, up-tempo pop-rock tune with a memorable keyboard hook.

The radio station wanted to include the track on a local-bands compilation (which also featured Twisted Sister, who enjoyed a brief but memorable run of success in the mid-to-late Eighties). "I never wanted to be part of it," recalled Jon. "I had the dream that I was gonna get a record deal, but suddenly all I was gonna get was one song on this *Home Grown* record. It's like somebody offering you a singles deal or an EP deal, which is what they used to do around here ten years ago. You'd go, 'Fuck this'. But eventually I got into that thing, thank goodness!"

While Jon was in the process of putting together a band to promote the local success of 'Runaway', one key member of Bon Jovi was waiting in the wings—guitarist Richie Sambora.

ENTER RICHIE

A local musician with a track record of minor bands in his wake (including the Screaming Mimis, the Bruce Foster Band, Duke Williams & The Extremes and The Message), Richie Sambora came from a background less exotic than Jon's but no less supportive—his parents bought him the necessary instruments and encouraged him as a musician.

"We were a working-class family and my Dad worked two jobs and my Mom also worked, so for them to be able to buy me those things was a big deal. First thing I did when I made any money was to retire them and buy them a home. They encouraged me and worked so hard to get me to where I wanted

Motley Crüe, sporting the glam rock look Bon Jovi toyed with then rejected.

All for one and one for all—the enduring Bon Jovi line-up.

was good. He had his own style, which wasn't ripped off from Eddie Van Halen—like all the other guitarists that were kicking around that year.

"At the time my guitarist was my neighbourhood friend, Dave Sabo (later to feature in Skid Row), but that band was only going to last for three weeks. Then 'Runaway', one of the songs I'd recorded, started to get played on New York radio stations and I needed to get a proper band together. Alec was earning a fortune playing bass in this covers band with Richie, our keyboard player.

"David was still at school [Juliard Music College] and our drummer Tico was between records with Frankie And The Knockouts [a melodic AOR—adult

to be, so I've tried to share everything with them."

Richie approached Jon at a concert to promote WAPT's *Home Grown* compilation and expressed an interest in joining the band—a suggestion Jon didn't take too seriously. "I've known Richie for about ten years," Jon told one interviewer in early 1993. "Back then he wanted to be in the band and I told him no way. In fact I told him to fuck off!

"Nah, our bass player Alec was playing in a bar band and he talked me into letting Richie come down and do his stuff. When I listened again I realized he

The boys are back in town, at home, on-stage!

orientated rock—outfit]. All of them came from what they were doing to my garage. They gave up a lot. In fact, Tico and Alec lost their wives because of it. I was very lucky, and there's no way I would have given up on this band and turned my back after everything we've been through.

"I put this band together around great guys rather than the greatest players. I wanted people who I could get along with; no egos in the band—even at club level. There were definitely better players than all of us, but not five personalities who were going to stick together as well as these did. Of course everyone had to be more than ample as players, but I knew the camaraderie of being on the road for a year at a time was going to be more important than anything."

CHANGE OF NAME

Jon Bongiovi wanted the band's name to have an ambiguous feel, and settled for a phonetic spelling— Bon Jovi—firstly because it was non-specific enough to carry no stereotypical heavy metal connotations, but also because it blurred the line between frontman and band. Could the other guys really matter if the band's star attraction had such prominent billing?

"I'm not egotistical," he reasoned. "I mean I'm confident about everything, but to have just sidemen

> **"RICHIE HAD HIS OWN STYLE, WHICH WASN'T RIPPED OFF FROM EDDIE VAN HALEN—LIKE ALL THE OTHER GUITARISTS THAT WERE KICKING AROUND THAT YEAR."**
> *Jon Bon Jovi*

Family fortunes? Jon on the town with his Dad.

> ## "WE ARE TRULY A FAMILY. MY MOTHER THINKS SHE HAS FOUR MORE SONS CALLED BON JOVI, BECAUSE IT'S VERY MUCH A TEAM."
> *Jon Bon Jovi*

you lack a vital ingredient. My guys put out 100 per cent every night too… We are truly a family. My mother thinks she has four more sons called Bon Jovi, because it's very much a team."

Once the JBJ./Sambora/Bryan (then still known as Rashbaum)/Such/Torres line-up had been established and 'Runaway' had done its thing, Jon rapidly secured a deal with PolyGram Records, in July 1983, and the

Rocking out with Jersey legend Little Steven, from Springsteen's E-Street Band.

Fashion victims: Bon Jovi always dressed to impress, but this would soon change.

band recorded their debut album, unimaginatively titled *Bon Jovi*, at the Power Station—the very same recording facility Jon had swept up and odd-jobbed for not so long before. He also, famously, found himself opening for ZZ Top at the famous Madison Square Garden in New York, before the album had even been released.

"I find it difficult to talk about the old albums because I haven't listened to them for so long," says Jon, in reflection. "These days, the only time I might hear something from those days is when I call our management office; they put me on hold and they're playing old Bon Jovi. Some of that stuff makes me smile and some of it makes me wince. But for the most part I look back on it fondly, because whatever we were doing was the best we could possibly be at the time."

FOND MEMORIES

"I remember it now simply because I'd finally got a record deal and I was in New York at the Power Station, sitting in the studio where the whole rock world and their mothers had been before, and now it was my turn. 'Runaway' and 'Shot Through The Heart' are the songs I'm still real proud of. On the other hand, 'She Don't Know Me' [written by Marc Avasec, of quirky AOR outfit Donnie Iris And The Cruisers] is a reminder not to record other people's material again."

Only a year after its release, Sambora was ready to admit, "We were so young as a band. We knew what we were doing but we still were produced and very easily led, and if the producer said to me, 'I don't like your guitar sound, change it!' I would just say, fine. This year it's more, 'Hey, wait a minute, this is the way I play'."

Richie takes a rest.

While no one in the band will go out on a limb to make great claims for the first album—"It had good heart," says Sambora, "even if we had a lot to learn at that point"—the ball had to start rolling somewhere. 'Runaway' gave them a US Top 40 single and the media began to pay attention to this good looking Jersey kid and his band.

It does no disservice to Bon Jovi to point out that they benefited from very fortuitous timing—plugging a gap in the hard-rock market that was just begging to be filled. In Europe, the influential rock critics at England's *Kerrang* magazine had long championed the cause of slick, American AOR—indeed, the presence of cult AOR artist Aldo Nova adding keyboards to the album track 'Breakout' stirred an early interest with the cognoscenti—but Jon Bon Jovi was the first

> **"IF YOU LOOK ON THE INSIDE OF THE ALBUM COVER, WE'RE JUST WEARING WHAT WE ARE WEARING ON THE STREET. WE'RE IMAGE CONSCIOUS, BUT IN A DIFFERENT WAY, AND I CERTAINLY PLAY DOWN ANY LOOK THAT THE BAND HAS."**
> *Jon Bon Jovi*

artist to really put a marketable face to the polished hard-rock variant; as well as injecting both heavier and poppier elements, giving AOR a fresher, more palatable, well-rounded feel.

A STAR IN THE MAKING

Meanwhile, in America, the hottest new rock acts were bigger on flash and shell-shocked bluster than on content—the likes of Quiet Riot and Motley Crüe

Shell-shocked rock rivals Motley Crüe.

had spearheaded a rush of young, popular heavy metal talent, but much of it (one-hit-album wonders Quiet Riot in particular) sounded as one-dimensional as it looked garish. Bon Jovi were more clean-cut for sure, but also took an early interest in craftsmanship that bands like the Crüe only developed a few albums into their careers (if at all).

Jon has since admitted that "we were the guys dressed in white, the people who could meet your sister and your mum, and still sink a few beers with the guys"—the no-nonsense good guys, in other words. But the rock establishment—and a sizeable chunk of the hard-rock audience—were holding out for just such a hero, and Bon Jovi gave them one.

Rock critic Paul Suter, when reviewing the album in *Kerrang*, noted that "Jon Bon Jovi has assembled a band of classic finesse and brutal strength… the material is dramatic and energetic, and blessed with a commerciality that should ensure plentiful sales and success."

Lavishing praise on Richie Sambora's "biting guitar firepower," Suter concluded that the band's debut was "truly an excellent package, and one already in the running for album of the year."

Even reading between the lines of critical hyperbole it was clear that the band had struck a powerful chord with the press. The album may sound naïve in 1993, even extremely unremarkable in

Jon's childhood sweetheart, Dorothea.

places, but in the context of what was going on in 1984, it was a breath of fresh air—an East Coast alternative to the excesses of West Coast bad-boy rock, with a star-in-the-making at the helm.

NOT JUST PRETTY BOYS

And make no mistake, Jon had that elusive star-quality—even if it was of the unrefined and pre-pubescent variety. The notion that Bon Jovi were pretty-boy pin-up rockers surfaced fairly early on, but always met with resistance from Jon: "If you look on the inside of the album cover, we're just wearing what we're wearing on the street. We're image conscious, but in a different way, and I certainly play down any look that the band has."

But no amount of protest could distract from the fact that Bon Jovi were quick to pick up a female following—they were not simply a guys' band. (Jon was even offered a major acting role, as the male lead in the film *Footloose*, the part that went to Kevin Bacon, before the album was released—an offer he rejected because what he wanted "to be known for was making records.")

A significant early review (from *Kerrang*) of the band opening for German hard rockers the Scorpions, on tour in America, pictured the group still finding their feet—"Jon Bon Jovi certainly has a pleasant voice, but lacks any charisma or charm. Taking elements from Jagger, [Aerosmith's Steven] Tyler and Rod Stewart, Bon Jovi… is never quite sure what direction to take first."

The reviewer concluded: "It all smacks of inexperience and suggests that Bon Jovi has yet to acquire the necessary tools to bolster his current, rather surprising success."

But with the band soon to arrive in Europe, supporting New York rock legends Kiss, the necessary road miles would soon be clocked up, with the band learning and developing with every concert played.

> **"JON BON JOVI HAS ASSEMBLED A BAND OF CLASSIC FINESSE AND BRUTAL STRENGTH…THE MATERIAL IS DRAMATIC AND ENERGETIC, AND BLESSED WITH A COMMERCIALITY THAT SHOULD ENSURE PLENTIFUL SALES AND SUCCESS."**
> *Paul Suter*

GETTING HOTTER

Starting a trend that was to haunt the band even in more successful days, album number two, 1985's *7800⁰ Fahrenheit*, was a rushed recording. "When the last Kiss tour came to an end for us we had four days off and then went straight into pre-production for the album," explained Jon. "We've really hustled, knowing that we had to keep in the public eye."

Even this early on, the band were on a roll from which they would receive little respite. In another interview, Jon claimed that "we have not been apart for more than a week at a time since last January [1984] when the first album came out."

Recording at Philadelphia's Warehouse studio, the band found themselves competing for the attention of producer Lance Quinn with Nils Lofgren (solo artist and sometime Neil Young collaborator, who,

ironically, replaced one of Jon's heroes, Little Steven, in Bruce Springsteen's E. Street Band).

Jon admitted that studio delays were down to his own desire to work with certain recording engineers. "We should have had the thing mixed down and ready by the time Lance had Nils Lofgren in his studio, only my schedules got mixed up."

BAND BONDING

Jon's first choice studio engineer, Larry Alexander (who had worked on the debut album), ducked out at the mixing stage to work with Duran Duran. By the time an acceptable replacement had been found (after one rejected mix) the band were recording during the daytime, while Nils Lofgren was using the same studio and producer at night (and even using

Flying the flag for classic U.S. rock.

> "WHEN THE LAST KISS TOUR CAME TO AN END FOR US WE HAD FOUR DAYS OFF AND THEN WENT STRAIGHT INTO PRE-PRODUCTION FOR THE ALBUM. WE'VE REALLY HUSTLED, KNOWING WE HAD TO KEEP IN THE PUBLIC EYE."
> *Jon Bon Jovi*

Bon Jovi's equipment to save time).

"There were a lot of legal hassles going on in our lives outside the band at the time. Tico and Alex got divorced, and the whole band was living in this little apartment in Philadelphia. My father brought round mattresses for us to sleep on, and we had a pot of spaghetti sauce in the freezer, and we just lived on that for a while. It might sound like a cliché, but this was the time when we were really starting to bond as a band," recalled Jon. Unfortunately, while the band were bonding, it wasn't just Tico and Alex who exprienced break-ups of relationships—Jon split with his long-term girlfriend, Dorothea (though the two have since reunited and married).

"'The Hardest Part Is The Night' is probably my favourite from that time, that and 'Only Lonely'.

"Hello England!"—Jon rocks British fans at the outdoor venue Castle Donington.

> "THERE WERE A LOT OF LEGAL HASSLES GOING ON IN OUR LIVES OUTSIDE THE BAND AT THE TIME. TICO AND ALEX GOT DIVORCED, AND THE WHOLE BAND WAS LIVING IN THIS LITTLE APARTMENT IN PHILADELPHIA."
> *Jon Bon Jovi*

Jon and Richie pull some shapes.

Some of the other songs I'm not so sure of," he has since admitted.

Hopes were riding high over this second release. The critics were looking for the band to consolidate on their well received first release and start to deliver something a little bit special. They were to be disappointed—the album was a patchy affair.

"This is a pale imitation of the Bon Jovi we have got to know and learnt to love," wrote Howard Johnson in *Kerrang*.

"There's a slight shift in approach, emphasis perhaps slanting towards bold (or clumsy, take your pick!), meatier chording," he noted, going on to concede that: "Jon Bon Jovi's shown he's got the right stuff." But the album, he decided, consisted mainly of "mediocre fare," and few would argue with that verdict.

FLYING TONIGHT

Even if the critics were a little unsure about the development of the band's fledgling pop-rock blend, few would disagree with the notion that Bon Jovi still had the makings of a classic hard-rock act with a brilliant career ahead of them. But if their supporters were becoming impatient, Jon was only too aware of the dangers of reaping too much, too soon.

In the wake of *Slippery When Wet*'s landslide victory, Jon mused: "I can't really complain about that album (*7800° Fahrenheit*); it was a rushed job but that was my fault, and in a way it was the perfect second step because it allowed us more time to build."

High flyers Bon Jovi take to the air.

And although they couldn't please the press with it, the album kept the band's upward momentum moving along nicely. Jon's enthusiasm more than painted over any cracks in their second outing.

"We're not 40-year old guys with toupees that pretend to believe in the kids and tell them, 'Oh, everything can be alright'!" he declared, back in 1985. "What do they know driving around in their Ferarris, living in mansions? They don't know what it's like to touch the kids in the front row because they don't do it any more… but we do!"

The idea of physical contact with the audience was

"THIS IS A PALE IMITATION OF THE JON BON JOVI WE HAVE GOT TO KNOW AND LEARNT TO LOVE."
Howard Johnson, Rock Critic

one that Jon was to come back to, time and again. Both in song (the dramatic *New Jersey* album opener, 'Lay Your Hands On Me') and through performance stunts like his infamous "flying" over the crowd during the *Slippery* and *New Jersey* tours.

"I love jumping in the crowd," he admitted at the height of *Slippery*-mania. "I always wished the guys did that when I was at those shows, you know, touched you kind of, said 'Hi', gave you the microphone. Those are the things I'd wished happened to me."

Soundchecking for the Farm Aid concert—Texas 1986.

Note the debris—plastic bottle throwing was a big feature of open-air concerts!

BETTER THE RATTS?

A fast developing canny knack for identifying exactly what an audience wanted and delivering just that and more was evident even in the adolescent *Fahrenheit* era.

Kerrang's Malcolm Dome, who had slated them on their first outing with the Scorpions, was forced to reconsider when he next watched the band touring with then-happening Los Angeles raunch 'n' rollers Ratt.

"His [Jon's] craft has now developed long past the infancy of imitation to the point of stylish individuality," read Dome's review of that era, adding, "he's now matured into a first-rate singer within his own limitations."

Touring America with Ratt gave Jon an opportunity to size up the opposition, so to speak. More than once, he's admitted that he considered Bon Jovi to be the better band, and he often found himself perplexed as to why Ratt were enjoying greater success.

If a competitive edge developed between the two bands, it wasn't a friendly one. "It was hell," Jon later explained. "Me and Stephen [Pearcy, Ratt's frontman] definitely didn't get along." Jon later overcame any rivalry to contribute backing vocals to the Ratt track 'Heads I Win, Tails You Lose'.

"I CAN'T REALLY COMPLAIN ABOUT *7800° FAHRENHEIT*; IT WAS A RUSHED JOB BUT THAT WAS MY FAULT AND IN A WAY IT WAS THE PERFECT SECOND STEP BECAUSE IT ALLOWED US MORE TIME TO BUILD."
Jon Bon Jovi

> **"WHAT I REMEMBER MOST OF ALL IS HOW SPOILED WE FELT WHEN WE CAME BACK FROM THE UK TOUR THAT YEAR. WE HAD HEADLINED THE DOMINION THEATRE IN LONDON, AND WE WANTED TO GO BACK TO THE STATES AND DO THE SAME THING OVER THERE."**
> *Jon Bon Jovi*

Bearded and burnt-out, but giving his all at UK's Castle Donington.

FASHION VICTIMS

For a while, Jon toyed with the notion that the key to putting Bon Jovi on a similar level with Ratt and Motley Crüe (who were both enjoying phenomenal success at the time) was to adopt a similar glam-metal image. "I remember thinking, you know, we gotta go out and rip our clothes up, we gotta go out and wear make-up, and we gotta go out and get the fake jewellery! This'll make us big…

"It took us a while to find ourselves, that's all. I

mean, you walk down the street in Jersey wearing make-up, man, you're going to get your ass kicked."

Motley Crüe thrived on a larger-than-life, stack-heeled horror-show look and Ratt personified Sunset Strip sleaziness, but Bon Jovi simply looked a little

> ## "I REMEMBER THINKING, YOU KNOW, WE GOTTA GO OUT AND RIP OUR CLOTHES UP, WE GOTTA GO OUT AND WEAR MAKE-UP, AND WE GOTTA GO OUT AND GET THE FAKE JEWELLERY! THIS'LL MAKE US BIG... IT TOOK US A WHILE TO FIND OURSELVES."
> *Jon Bon Jovi*

over-dressed in sequined stage-costumes and heavily-hairsprayed coiffures. It would be a few years yet before they would appear in nothing more ornate than old jeans and T-shirts, but their experiments with the extremes of rock fancy dress were not judged successful.

ON THE UK BILL

Despite some regrettably amusing attempts at super-star finery, they would never again spend as much

Top rock buddies, Jon with Joe Elliott of Def Leppard pose in relaxed mode.

Tired and emotional on tour: playing music hot as an exploding volcano took its toll.

time fretting over appearances. "We said, this sucks. I'm uncomfortable in these clothes. I hate these fucking heels, I want my sneakers back!"

In Europe the band had already attained headline status—albeit at smaller halls, like London's Dominion Theatre, rather than better known venues like the Hammersmith Odeon. But the decision to tour as headliner (with Canadian chanteuse Lee Aaron in support) was another indication of the band's serious, long-term agenda. If you want to be big, they seemed to be saying, you've got to think big and look big.

The band later appeared at England's prestigious Monsters Of Rock festival, in a more-than-respectable third on the bill slot (two years later, in 1987, they'd return as headliners).

The Dominion show in London was a key appearance for the band—it was a sell-out which confirmed that the band hadn't lost their buzz, even if 7800° *Fahrenheit* had failed to ignite (despite its title, which represented the temperature of an exploding volcano).

"*Fahrenheit* went Gold in the US, but what I remember most of all is how spoiled we felt when we came back from the UK tour that year. We had headlined the Dominion Theatre in London, and we wanted to go back to the States and do the same thing over there."

THE SLIPPERY ROAD TO SUPERSTARDOM

We never knew it was going to be anything special while we were still recording it—at the time, we thought everything we did was special!" laughs Jon, when asked about the *Slippery When Wet* phenomenon.

With a new production team of Bruce Fairbairn and engineer/mixer Bob Rock and contributions from a significant outside songwriter, *Slippery When Wet* was one of the significant rock albums of the Eighties. This time, critics who'd waited for Jon to finally take up the mantle of hard-rock superstar were handsomely rewarded.

Malcolm Dome, writing in *Kerrang*, noted: "What it sees is the band maturing and coming into their own without the aid of any hyping crutches… they seem to have learnt from the mistakes made on the second album and used this to drastically improve on the first LP."

And, just as the debut album had put Jon in the right place at the right time, *Slippery When Wet* enjoyed some beneficial synchronicity, at least with the use of videos.

Alec pumps it up on bass.

No turning back for Jon now.

"I think this band is almost responsible for the 'big, live video'! The patented Bon Jovi style video. There is this image that this is a big party band, good lookin' guys that write hooks, but there's a lot more to this band," protested Jon. But there was no denying the fact that MTV couldn't get enough of that patented JBJ video experience—all slick editing, glossy concert lighting, flashing pyrotechnics and, in the middle of it all, the band flashing teeth and tossing manes of hair, projecting good-time vibes and loving every minute of it. But the video clips were only icing on the cake—the filling came with a brace of bold, dynamic rock tunes that turned heads, opened ears and ultimately sold by the truck-load.

CHILD-LIKE

Slippery contained not one but two up-beat chart smashes—'You Give Love A Bad Name' and 'Living On A Prayer'—both co-written by Desmond Child, a songwriter who had previously worked with Kiss (whose Paul Stanley recommended him to Jon). In the aftermath, as well as working on future records with Jon, Child became an in-demand collaborator, co-writing with the likes of Aerosmith and Alice Cooper. There were some, however, who felt that Child was guilty of recycling a formula of 'whoa-whoa'-type choruses and poppy hooklines into virtually everything he worked on.

Said Jon: "A lot of people thought there was a formula to that record but there wasn't. I'd started working with Desmond and between us and the band we just came up with the best material we'd written up till then. It was very much a learning experience and we were on a high for months afterwards.

"He gets a lot of heat these days because he wrote with a number of other artists and none of the songs he wrote for them were Number 1 hits, so people thought he was becoming a whore—that he'd loan himself out to anybody if the price was right. Don't forget, a few years ago the guy was barely making enough money to live. And, whatever you might think of his songs, Desmond remains a great songwriter. In 1986 he definitely taught me the next level of songwriting, and I wouldn't hesitate to work with him again."

LEARNING THE LIVE THING

The next level of songwriting took Bon Jovi to the next level of stardom—a level few bands ever come close to. 'Wanted Dead Or Alive', a moody,

Slippery success: you can have your cake and eat it when the hits started rolling in.

atmospheric track which compared the band's travelling troubadour lifestyle to the classic images of the cowboys of the Wild West, proved that the band were capable of more than metallic pop tunes and provided an appropriate soundtrack for their heavy promotional chores, as they plunged headlong into their longest tour yet.

Slippery's 18-million-sale success worldwide even allowed Jon leeway to reflect on his fame-hungry youth and the single-minded drive that was required to take Bon Jovi to the brink of international stardom and beyond.

"To steal a phrase from Eddie Murphy," he told *Kerrang*, "when the first album came out I was like an 18-year-old kid fucking. It was all very quick with no rhythm. There I was thinking I was a star and nobody

And for my next trick... Jon as caped crusader.

"WE NEVER KNEW IT WAS GOING TO BE ANYTHING SPECIAL WHILE WE WERE STILL RECORDING IT. AT THE TIME, WE THOUGHT EVERYTHING WE DID WAS SPECIAL!"
Jon Bon Jovi

knew me! The second album came along and I began to understand how to work the live thing, I started to learn the moves. It was only when we headlined Castle Donington [Monsters of Rock] in 1988 that I really felt in control."

Even though the Castle Donington show had been pivotal in terms of cementing the band's status as one of the super-groups of the decade, it arrived at a time when the strain of constant touring and promotional duties was beginning to show—literally.

The band were physically exhausted, and Jon's appearance (raggedy beard, sunglasses-after-dark and, for stage gear what one magazine described as "the contents of an Oxfam shop") may have been an attempt to disguise the fatigue, but it only made it all the more obvious.

GOING INTO ORBIT

The show was, nonetheless, well received, *Kerrang* calling it a "dominating tour de force" and that

They're back! Facing the press.

> ## "IT SEES THE BAND MATURING AND COMING INTO THEIR OWN WITHOUT THE AID OF ANY HYPING CRUTCHES...THEY SEEM TO HAVE LEARNT FROM THE MISTAKES MADE ON THE SECOND ALBUM AND USED THIS TO DRASTICALLY IMPROVE ON THE FIRST LP."
> *Malcolm Dome, Rock Critic*

"technically the band are brilliant. They've built on years of listening to the rock heritage, applying musical skills undreamt of not so long ago". Again, what may seem like critical perspective gone hopelessly awry starts to make more sense when viewed within the context of the rock scene that Bon Jovi had reached the peak of.

By the standards of their peers, Bon Jovi were technically more than competent, and all the more effective for not ramming virtuosity down people's throats, as is the trend in metal circles—whereever

Tico, the crazy Cuban, does his stuff.

possible, Bon Jovi kept any instrumental panache within a solid, song-based context.

In another attempt to put his career into perspective, Jon noted that, circa 1984, "our idea of the big time was if the record company would take us out to dinner." By the second album the idea had expanded: "We had a little bit more success, we were third on the bill at Donington, nice cruise control. The *Slippery* thing came out and this bitch just took off. That was the last time anyone saw us for about four years, we were orbiting.

"We trudged on, glad to be there," he reflects after Donington, "not realizing that we were burned. You'd think that someone around us would have mentioned it. It was the worst time of my life. I needed a vacation so badly, but I still gave Donington everything I had."

Even exhaustion couldn't stop Jon from indulging in one of his favourite pastimes—putting as many musicians on-stage for the encores as possible. Thus, Paul Stanley of Kiss, Dee Snider of Twisted Sister and Iron Maiden's Bruce Dickinson all joined the band for 'We're An American Band'—Bruce using the opportunity to announce that his band would be taking the headline slot at Donington in a year's time.

'Born To Run'—Jersey superstar Bruce the Boss strutting his stuff in concert.

"I THINK THIS BAND IS ALMOST RESPONSIBLE FOR THE 'BIG...LIVE...VIDEO'! THE PATENTED BON JOVI STYLE VIDEO . THERE IS THIS IMAGE THAT THIS IS A BIG PARTY BAND, GOOD LOOKIN' GUYS THAT WRITE HOOKS, BUT THERE'S A LOT MORE TO THIS BAND."

Jon Bon Jovi

Richie sweats it out with another hot solo.

Such jam sessions inevitably steal a little of the main attraction's limelight, but Jon—for all his vanity, real and imagined—knows that it's moments like this that the fans cherish, and is happy to spread a little of the glory around.

The tour—ironically dubbed 'The Tour Without End'—continued for three more months before it finished, after a gruelling 130 shows. The band were hoping for a well-earned rest, but four months later were back in the studio.

THE SYNDICATE

The album title actually has nothing to do with the place," explained Richie Sambora, when the band released album number four, *New Jersey*. "It's about an attitude. It's like Liverpool. If you grew up there you have a Liverpool attitude. It colours your life, and with this record we're trying to bring the fans closer to us, so they know what we're about… It's an attitude of friendship and camaraderie and it's very 'street'."

Bon Jovi were keen not to simply churn out *Slippery II: The Sequel*, but that didn't stop them from returning to the winning Fairbairn/Rock recording team at Little Mountain Studios in Vancouver, Canada. "It worked last time, I think it'll do well again, because he [Bruce Fairbairn] did a fine job… I think he's great and that he's gotten better," said Jon.

"The *Slippery* tour ended in Hawaii and we stayed there a while because everyone needed a rest," says Jon. "Then, one by one we all left, apart from Richie who stayed there for about a month. We didn't do anything for three or four weeks then the phone calls started to change from 'Whatcha doin' today?' to 'Hey, I got this neat hook!' Then we demoed the first batch of songs. There were a couple of good ones in

there but we really started to feel the pressure then because we didn't have the amazing song.

"There was this real fear of not being able to write 'Bad Name' again. We sat in the house and wrote this song called 'Love Is War', and it sounded great, but I wanted to write 'Bad Name' so much it came out with exactly the same chord progression. Richie was saying, 'Don't worry about it, we'll get back in the groove'. And I'm walking about the house yelling, 'I gotta pay for this place, we gotta write some fucking hot songs!' Then we started on the second batch and they came flooding out."

Jon walks this way with Tyler and Perry from Aerosmith.

Arriving together before the big bust-up, Bon Jovi and Motley Crüe jet in to Moscow.

Bon Jovi Manager Doc McGhee would sell the jacket off your back.

"THE ALBUM TITLE ACTUALLY HAS NOTHING TO DO WITH THE PLACE. *NEW JERSEY'S* ABOUT AN ATTITUDE. IT'S LIKE LIVERPOOL. IF YOU GREW UP THERE YOU HAVE A LIVERPOOL ATTITUDE, IT COLOURS YOUR LIFE, AND WITH THIS RECORD WE'RE TRYING TO BRING THE FANS CLOSER TO US, SO THEY KNOW WHAT WE'RE ABOUT...IT'S AN ATTITUDE OF FRIENDSHIP AND CAMARADERIE AND IT'S VERY 'STREET'."
Richie Sambora

Soviet stage security lines up to protect the band from rampaging fans.

TOO GOOD-TIME

The album's working title was *Sons Of Beaches*, but the band were concious of a need to display a little growth—*Sons Of Beaches* could only really be interpreted as a good-time title for a good-time

album: "I mean *Slippery*'s greatest attribute was that they wouldn't let us use the cover that we wanted." It was a girl's bust, barely concealed by a *Slippery* T-shirt, which does appear on Japanese copies of the album. "At the eleventh hour we had to make a cover, a black cover with my finger writing 'Slippery When Wet'. The greatest thing about it—that we never knew till now—was that it left it all to your imagination.

"And so with this, *Sons Of Beaches* would make you think, 'well, I have to have fun listening to this record. I have to think that the band are really funny, that it's Summer and all that'."

The idea was ditched in favour of *New Jersey*, which came with problems of its own. "I was never compared to that guy [Bruce Springsteen] until I called the fourth album *New Jersey*," complained Jon in one interview. "And if I made one mistake in my career. calling that record *New Jersey* was it! That's what led to these Springsteen comparisons and ever since then I was wondering what the fuck it was all about."

Bon Jovi and Motley Crüe rub shoulders with Russian rockers Gorky Park.

Rocking blonde Lita Ford who opened for Bon Jovi on the first leg of the New Jersey tour.

> "I WAS NEVER COMPARED TO BRUCE SPRINGSTEEN UNTIL I CALLED THE FOURTH ALBUM *NEW JERSEY*. AND IF I MADE ONE MISTAKE IN MY CAREER. CALLING THAT RECORD *NEW JERSEY* WAS IT! THAT'S WHAT LED TO THESE SPRINGSTEEN COMPARISONS AND EVER SINCE THEN I WAS WONDERING WHAT THE FUCK IT WAS ALL ABOUT."
> *Jon Bon Jovi*

BLOOD BROTHERS

He prefers the notion that Bon Jovi are carrying on in the tradition of Phil Lynott and Thin Lizzy with "heavier, guitar oriented storytelling", but, despite Jon's protests, there were moments on the *New Jersey* album that could only be described as Springsteen-esque, in particular 'Blood On Blood'. A pumping, exhilarating, wide-screen narrative, it gave Bruce's familiar galloping 'Born To Run'-style sound a

'Blood On Blood'—heralded a new depth in song writing.

metallic edge and a pop sensibility, while dealing with Jon's own adolescence and coming-of-age.

He refers to the characters in the song: "Bobby and Danny are two guys I know who used to live in Jersey, we used to hang out. I think that anybody out there who had buddies when you were about 13 you swore were your friends forever, y'know? And, although I haven't seen these guys for years and years, I still remember when I was 13, so I started writing a song, and I hope it's one of our best we've ever done."

Behind the Iron Curtain: Russian band Gorky Park enjoy their 15 minutes of fame.

To borrow a Springsteen-ism, 'Blood On Blood' was the most memorable example yet of Jon's obsession with the ties that bind.

"I've read it a hundred times over the years," he shrugs. "I pick up a magazine and someone is saying we write these clichéd adolescent lyrics about friendship. And I think, shit, friendship's always been pretty important to me.

"And these social issues people talk about, I know when I was 16 or 17, I was more worried about getting a car, getting laid and making my first buck than I was about who was going to be the next President of the United States, you know? And that's what I write about in my songs, because that's what I've experienced. I've never wanted to run for president."

THE FANS MAKE IT

'Blood On Blood' was representative of a new depth in the band's songwriting—overall in the album the band display a classy maturity without sacrificing the energetic pop flourishes which had made *Slippery* such a success. 'Bad Medicine', with its exuberant dummy-ending and the foot-tapping 'Born To Be My Baby' (both composed by the hit-making combination of JBJ, Sambora and Desmond Child) provided the necessary hit-single angles, while 'Stick To Your Guns' and the throw-away mono-recording 'Ride Cowboy Ride' further developed the cowboy mythology of 'Wanted Dead Or Alive'.

> **"WE KNOW IT'S NOT THE SONGS THAT ARE IMPORTANT AS MUCH AS HOW YOU FEEL AT THE END OF THEM, THAT'S WHAT ROCK 'N' ROLL IS, IT'S MORE OF AN EMOTIONAL RELEASE THAN A MUSIC FORM."**
> *Jon Bon Jovi*

'Lay Your Hands On Me', the album's opener, was a dramatic, thumping, percussive anthem and would probably have sounded like arrogant self aggrandizement were it not for Jon's endearingly affectionate rapport with his audience.

It was, according to Sambora "essentially saying 'check us out, here we are, touch us. We're going to make you part of this because you made it happen'."

Jon reckons it "says we're still accessible. It's an opener and it's meant to be that—just put your needle down on the record."

Whenever possible, Bon Jovi have previewed new material to teenage baby-sitters, local kids hanging out near the studio or any other available youngsters who

Bon Jovi unplugged.

might have what the band consider vital input to make.

"It's like a relationship between family, between business partners. We've always paid attention to what our audience thinks," explains Jon. "They picked two songs which wouldn't have been on the album otherwise: 'Stick To Your Guns' and 'Wild Is The Wind'—we were going to save them for the next record."

The fans, he notes are the ones who buy the records and they had valid reasons for wanting those

"*NEW JERSEY* WILL BE THE FIRST CONTEMPORARY WESTERN ROCK ALBUM RELEASED IN RUSSIA. AND THIS IS OFFICIAL, IT'S NOT THE BLACK-MARKET. THE STATE OWNED MELODIA RECORDS LABEL IS RELEASING *NEW JERSEY*. NO BEATLES, NO STONES, JUST US."
Jon Bon Jovi

Young guns of stage and screen unite, as Jon hangs out with the stars of Young Guns II.

songs to be included. "They liked the emotional content, and we know it's not the songs that are important as much as how you feel at the end of them—that's what rock 'n' roll is, it's more of an emotional release than a music form."

TRYING TO HIDE AWAY

Although the band had barely recovered from the rigors of the *Slippery When Wet* tours, *New Jersey* did not seem to suffer musically—if anything was deteriorating, it was the band's personal lives (or lack of them). Considering the fact that Jon was simultaneously involved in his most intensive bout of talent scouting yet (working with Skid Row—a

Despite their involvement with anti-drug campaigns, the lads enjoyed a beer or two.

> **"THE MAKE A DIFFERENCE FOUNDATION DEALS WITH DRUG, ALCOHOL AND SUBSTANCE ABUSE. THE RUSSIANS HAVE A PROBLEM WITH ALCOHOL OVER THERE, AND IT WAS A WAY THAT THE RUSSIAN GOVERNMENT WOULD SANCTION THE SHOW, ACTUALLY LET IT HAPPEN."**
> *Jon Bon Jovi*

coat down to my ankles hiding as much of my body as I can, my hair's as long as it can possibly be."

But his only escape route, ironically, involved immersing himself in even more work. Promoting *New Jersey*, the band played a massive 237 dates. When he was asked if their schedule would keep the band on the road for two years, Jon admitted: "I keep hearing that too, but every time I confront Doc (McGhee—the band's manager) with it he kind of mumbles something under his breath and leaves the room. But I know it's scheduled to go right through 1989."

Tour highlights included Jon appearing with Lita

Richie jams with one-time girlfriend Bekka Bramlet.

project dealt with in the With Friends And Alone chapter) and dealing with the burden of following-up the *Slippery* phenomenon, it's probably fair to say that he, at least, had no personal life. With a degree of prompting from manager Doc McGhee, Jon had become a full-blown workaholic.

In an attempt to analyze his own body-language, Jon has since noted that, on the inner-sleeve band photo for *New Jersey*, the last thing he wanted to do was be him. "I had my back to the camera, a long

"Thank you very much and goodnight!"

Ford (who opened for Bon Jovi on the first leg of the tour) at the female rocker's London Marquee show, Steven Tyler and Joe Perry of Aerosmith making their first British apperance in years to play 'Walk This Way' with Bon Jovi at their massive Milton Keynes Bowl show and, at the end of the tour, Jimmy Page of Led Zeppelin jamming with Richie at a special charity concert at London's Hammersmith Odeon.

As ever, this was the band who loved to jam.

THE BAND OF HYPOCRITES

Controversy is not a word that readily comes to mind when reviewing Jon Bon Jovi's career, but there was more than a hint of it in the air when the band

Thanks for the music: Jon meets Les Paul, designer of the classic guitar that bears his name.

"**THE GREAT THING ABOUT BEING AT A FESTIVAL WHERE ALL BANDS ARE EQUAL IS THAT ANYTHING IS FAIR GAME. BUT I DID NOT SET OFF THE PYRO, MY CREW DID NOT SET OFF THE PYRO...UNFORTUNATELY MOTLEY CRÜE LOST A GREAT MANAGER BECAUSE THEY THINK THAT PYRO WAS THE REASON THAT WE WENT OVER SO WELL.**"
Jon Bon Jovi

Jeff Beck, guitar slinger who featured on Jon's film soundtrack LP.

took part in the Moscow Peace Festival.

In the break between *Slippery When Wet* and *New Jersey*, band manager 'Doc' McGhee was convicted on charges of smuggling $40,000 (£26,600) of marijuana. Despite receiving a five-year suspended sentence, he was fined a mere $15,000 (£10,000)—due, perhaps, to his willingness to become involved in a major community service project.

This snowballed into two concerts in August of 1989 at Moscow's 140,000-capacity Olympic Stadium, by Doc McGhee's roster of managerial charges—Bon Jovi, the Scorpions, Motley Crüe, Skid Row—as well as rock legend Ozzy Osbourne and some local Russian acts.

While the rock stars involved were undoubtedly well-qualified to highlight the dangers of drink and drug abuse, there was a feeling that they were less than perfect role models—bassist Nikki Sixx had once been briefly declared clinically dead during a heroin overdose, while intoxicated frontman Vince Neil had been involved in a motoring accident which caused the death of one of his passengers, 'Razzle' of the Scandinavian glam-rock band Hanoi Rocks. Like McGhee, he, too, had received lenient sentencing from the courts.

Another participant, Ozzy Osbourne—the former Black Sabbath singer, who has enjoyed a successful but controversial solo career—had made no secret of a life-long battle with alcoholism for which he could claim only partial success.

Bon Jovi stablemates Skid Row, meanwhile, were already proving to be an erratic, electrifying but barely controllable outfit during their short stint in the public eye (these days frontman Sebastian Bach is a vocal campaigner for the legalization of marijuana in the US). Over-all, any cynicism the event created was probably at least partially deserved.

BEHIND THE IRON CURTAIN

The festival was also used as a springboard to launch (or at least attempt to launch) Gorky Park, a Russian rock outfit who JBJ and McGhee relocated to the West. In any event, Gorky Park made virtually no impact with their Western debut (an album for the PolyGram label), though Jon was proudly able to announce that *New Jersey* "will be the first contemporary Western rock album released in Russia". And it was official. "It's not the blackmarket.

"Who is this old guy?" It's country star Willie Nelson, meeting Jon at Farm Aid.

Another Young Guns collaborator, Elton John, comparing hats with Jon.

The state owned Melodia Records label is releasing *New Jersey*. No Beatles, no Stones, just us."

A landmark boast, but one which highlighted the way in which the charitable intentions of the Foundation were unavoidably intertwined with promotional and commercial opportunities.

At the time, Jon explained: "The Make A Difference Foundation deals with drug, alcohol and substance abuse. The Russians have a problem with alcohol over there, and it was a way that the Russian government would sanction the show, actually let it happen."

Although previous western artists, including Billy Joel and Elton John, had gone behind the then-very-real Iron Curtain, nothing had been attempted on this scale before.

Even before the festival took place, when asked if a

"Hey, pretty woman", sez Jon to Julia Roberts.

similar concert was feasible anywhere else in the world, Jon quipped: "Everyone's egos wouldn't fit anywhere else in the world!"

SHOW-STEALER

It was a comment that may well have come back to haunt him. Although Bon Jovi topped the bill and appeared last, the event was promoted as a co-headlining event. Just prior to the first gig, Ozzy Osbourne had declared his unwillingness to play fourth on the bill, under Motley Crüe—Jon, at the time had offered his closing slot to Ozzy, until Motley acquiesced (though Ozzy and Motley's performances were switched back to reflect the original billing when the event was broadcast on TV in the US). But the real problem over status came when Motley Crüe took exception to a firework from the closing display that was inadvertently ignited during one of Bon Jovi's closing songs.

The Russian audience, unfamiliar with most of the acts bar Ozzy and the Scorpions, had been subdued in their responses on the first night. On the second, Jon had already come close to stealing the show by dressing as a Russian soldier and arriving on stage by sneaking though the middle of the crowd. The firework, which Motley Crüe considered to be unfair use of show-stealing pyrotechnics, was the last straw—Motley 's Tommy Lee punched Doc McGhee and the band stormed off, giving notice of their desire to obtain new management.

"The great thing about being at a festival where all bands are equal is that anything is fair game," Jon commented after the event. Even so, he was adamant: "I did not set off the pyro, my crew did not set off the pyro, unfortunately they lost a great manager because they think that pyro was the reason that we went over so well."

MAKING THE DIFFERENCE

There was an album to tie in with the concerts, *Stairway To Heaven/Highway To Hell*, featuring various Make A Difference participants, covering songs by artists whose deaths had been linked to drink or drug use (Bon Jovi contributed 'The Boys Are Back In Town' by Thin Lizzy's Phil Lynott). But, several years on, the Make A Difference Foundation, it seems, has been wound down, and Jon (who has since severed all ties with McGhee) prefers an ambiguous stance to inquiries about the validity of the situation.

"I certainly supported it and him to the hilt," he reflected on the European leg of the *Keep The Faith* tour. "I thought going to Russia to do that was a great thing. I was also making speeches in High Schools in North Carolina, so I felt like being part of the Make A Difference Foundation was a real positive cause that related to our audience."

ALONE & WITH FRIENDS

With the first two albums we were on this nice easy course and things were going well, steadily climbing. Then the third album was like a rocket ship, way beyond anyone's expectations, and when that was over we jumped back in to do *New Jersey*. And that kept us on the treadmill, with never an opportunity to get off.

"It was only after *New Jersey* that we'd admit we were tired. Then we knew it was time to take a couple of years off for ourselves; Doc, my manager, told me I'd never manage to take two years off, and

Richie's idol, Eric "Slowhand" Clapton.

walking out of his office I had to admit to myself that I didn't have the faintest idea what I was going to do."

What Jon did, in the end, wouldn't be considered a holiday by most people. He admits, "Recovering from 16 months and 237 shows doesn't happen overnight. It takes about three or four weeks before you're not looking at the clock at nine o'clock wondering if it's time to go on yet.

"It's a nice feeling for a change, just to go home, see your own bed, put the suitcase away and know that you won't have to look at it for a while."

There was talk of a live double-album. "It won't just be a collection of songs, it'll be pretty different... we've got cover-songs, horn sections in, and what have you. I think a live album should be different, it should show what this band is about, the versatility."

Jon claimed to be the instigator of regular set-changes. "Lighting men and sound men and guitar techs get pissed off. But the band need it! We change the set around in the middle, the ballads were flexible, the cover songs were flexible. We often changed the opening track—I remember we opened with 'Wanted Dead Or Alive' one night. Everybody went crazy on me, but I was in the mood to start acoustically."

Friendlier days: Tommy Kiefer (Cinderella), Snake Sabo (Skid Row), Jon and Sebastian Bach (Skid Row) before the relationships skidded out of control.

IT WAS A NEAR THING

In the end, though, nothing came of live-record plans. "They gave me the tapes when I came home," says Jon, "and I tried to listen to them but I couldn't. I wanted to be away from it more."

Meanwhile, the press started to speculate that Bon Jovi were on the point of splitting. Tico was erroneously reported to have left the band, then Richie was the focus of similar speculation. While denials were issued all-round, cracks in the band's public image were beginning to show.

With individual members out of contact with each other, the press reports only added fuel to the fire while the band deny that any split ever took place they have been forced to concede that they came very, very close.

At the height of the "Bon Jovi to split" hysteria, Jon took the bizarre step of lashing out at the press for focusing mainly on Richie to the detriment of the rest of the band. "Everyone gives Richie a lot of attention—and well deserved it is, he's a fine musician and a fine singer—but I really don't feel it's fair to harp on about him all the time because it was us and the band.

"For the first two albums, he never co-wrote any of the singles. Dave Bryan co-wrote the singles. It

Guitar-man Richie takes a well-earned rest.

was Dave and I who did it. Richie came in on the third album when he had begun to understand the way I write."

Even if Bon Jovi was a band of equals, the fact that it bears his name makes it clear that this is not the case—Jon would still be more equal than most. In July 1990 he admitted that: "Right now things are not happy in the Bon Jovi camp, that's for sure. I don't want the band to break up," he stressed, but he also seemed to be paving the way for just such an event. "I think if Richie left the band he'd be stupid, but if he leaves, no big deal. The band will still continue."

BLAZE OF GLORY

In more recent times, Jon has attempted to continue spreading the limelight around a little, telling *Metal CD* magazine's Mark Blake that "the focus on the band has always fallen on me and Richie, because we represent that typical singer/guitarist partnership. But this band has always been about five people and I don't want to throw the spotlight on Richie alone."

But the spotlight fell firmly on the pair of them as they each embarked upon solo records.

The title emblazoned across the cover of Jon's solo album was a complex one—*Blaze Of Glory: Songs Written And Performed By Jon Bon Jovi, Inspired By The Film Young Guns II*. But it was a complex release—part

Richie strikes guitar hero pose number 372.

soundtrack record, part concept album. Jon fought shy of the notion that it was a solo album—if he was going to do one of those, he explained, he'd have written about a wider range of topics. Originally asked to write the title track to the Brat-pack Western sequel, he said: "Great, thanks, I'm pleased because I enjoy those kind of movies, but I'm free so I'll write you another one."

Even so, there was no denying that the East Coast boy was getting increasingly steeped in the mythology of the Wild West.

His life, he said, is like the way he wrote 'Wanted Dead Or Alive'. "I feel that you ride into town, you don't know where the fuck you are. You're with your 'gang'; stealing money; getting what you can off any girl that'll give it to you; drinking as much of the free alcohol as you can and being gone before the law catches you.

"Before someone wakes you up from this wonderful dream and says, 'You're going to jail'. Because it's not the real world I'm living in, it's a dream sequence, a big fucking wet dream."

ON SET

One song turned into two, then three, then four. PolyGram wanted an album tie-in but, Jon confessed, he didn't fancy the idea of four of his songs being

Out on the town: Richie and Cher together.

Tico in a quieter moment.

used as the main selling point on a record made up of contributions from lesser known bands from the PolyGram roster. So he ended up with a full-length album of material inspired by the *Young Guns II* story—even though not all of them made it into the film (in the end, only two were included). He even got a small acting role.

"It was like a fantasy, y'know, you get paid to rub dirt on your face and shoot guns! But don't blink or you'll miss me, cause it's only there for a second. I get killed."

Recording *Young Guns II* gave Jon the opportunity to work with some serious celebrity guests—the album features rock guitar legend Jeff Beck, as well as cameo appearances by Elton John and Little Richard.

"I found the whole experience of doing the soundtrack very rewarding. I wrote it all myself, I produced it, and I also had the chance to work with people like Jeff Beck—something I could never have imagined happening when I first started out.

"'Blaze of Glory' was the big hit, but 'Santa Fe' is probably the best track on the album. Right now another solo album doesn't figure in my plans. However satisfying an experience it was at the time, there's still that vague feeling of loneliness when you have a hit on your own and you're used to sharing it

"DOC, MY MANAGER, TOLD ME I'D NEVER MANAGE TO TAKE TWO YEARS OFF, AND WALKING OUT OF HIS OFFICE, I HAD TO ADMIT TO MYSELF THAT I DIDN'T HAVE THE FAINTEST IDEA WHAT I WAS GOING TO DO."
Jon Bon Jovi

Jon stretches those famed vocal chords.

"EVERYONE GIVES RICHIE A LOT OF ATTENTION—AND WELL DESERVED IT IS, HE'S A FINE MUSICIAN AND A FINE SINGER—BUT I REALLY DON'T FEEL IT'S FAIR TO HARP ON ABOUT HIM ALL THE TIME BECAUSE IT WAS US AND THE BAND."

Jon Bon Jovi

with the band, Jon admitted after the release."

He also claimed that it helped him appreciate the talent within the band. "I've come to realize through playing with many different musicians that Richie is a really creative guitarist, that Dave is a much better keyboard player than I ever thought he was, and that Tico is the only drummer for me."

Blaze Of Glory was a massive hit for Jon, while the album allowed him to experiment with country, blues and soul influences and experiment with various moods outside of the Bon Jovi format. Some critics said the songs ran out of steam by comparison to the consistently strong *New Jersey*, but from the angle of a break from the treadmill, the album could easily be considered a success.

BLUESMAN SAMBORA

Richie's solo outing, *Stranger In This Town*, may have failed to accrue quite so many album sales—or a major hit single for that matter—but it was, in some ways, a more rounded, satisfying affair, reaching a slightly older audience.

"For the last four and a half years in Bon Jovi I've basically worked on just two albums' worth of material—and then we went on the road and played 15 of 'em, so for that time my parameters of music was just 15 songs deep. It didn't leave me much space

More Jersey jammin', this time with Springsteen's sax-man, Clarence Clemmons, and Jon's old buddy, Southside Johnny.

"RIGHT NOW, IN JULY 1990...THINGS ARE NOT HAPPY IN THE BON JOVI CAMP, THAT'S FOR SURE."
Jon Bon Jovi

to expand as either a writer or a musician," he told one reporter.

Like Jon, he had a superstar guitarist and former Yardbird in to trade guitar licks—Eric Clapton to Jon's Jeff Beck; and like Jon he had a theme of sorts to build his album around, creating for himself the persona of "Mr. Bluesman".

"My album was all about finding myself again," said Sambora. "All those years of unrelenting pressure on the road had left me burned out."

Richie was more or less able to name his price when it came to recording *Stranger In This Town*—PolyGram's contract was with Jon, not the band, so Sambora found himself in the unique position of being a high-profile member of a major international rock group without a record deal to his name.

In the end he decided to stay with PolyGram,

Fairground attraction—Jon and the boys circa New Jersey.

School's out for Jon and Alice Cooper.

noting that he was able "to ask the record company for a superb amount of money, so I was able to stop and smell the roses and really get to be a better guitar player."

He constantly described the album as "dark". "I'm a bit of an old hippy," he told one interviewer. "When I was a kid I used to rehearse down in my mother's basement with my garage bands. I'd light candles and incense, drink beer and do psychedelic music... When we did the pre-production for this record we did it in Tico's basement and did the same thing—lit loads candles and incense... We recreated that kind of innocence where it was great to play again."

A DREAM OF ERIC

Aiming for a less contemporary sound than the Bon Jovi albums had contained, he said that he wanted to make a modern day record with the feelings and emotions of the late Sixties and early Seventies. "It was important to go and visit my roots and the origins of why I became a musician."

His explorations obviously meant a lot to him: "There was a time frame in which people wanted me to get it done so that I could get back to the band, which I ignored, basically.

"I said, 'Look, man, I pretty much gave up my life to this band for ten years, it's gonna be done when it's done and that's it'. I had to lay down the law and become a little selfish for the first time in my life."

The song 'Mr. Bluesman' was, he said, about "a young boy who wanted to play guitar—me wanting to be Eric [Clapton]." In the end, Richie got Clapton to play on the track, an experience he'd often dreamed about. A couple of the other songs dated back to pre-Bon Jovi days and he let it be known that "my heart is all over this record."

SOLO TOURS AND WORK

Jon kept a low profile, touring with the minimum of fuss as an anonymous member of his old hero Southside Johnny's back-up band (playing to crowds as small as 200 people at some venues) after the release of *Young Guns*. But Richie set out on a proper American solo tour to promote his album—backed by veteran session players like Tony Levin and his fellow Jovi-ites David Bryan and Tico Torres.

"The guy's a damn good frontman," reported rock critic Paul Suter of his Los Angeles concert, "his relaxed, friendly approach masking any trepidation he may have had over this solo outing… to his credit, Sambora commands attention and keeps it."

As well as his own solo material, Richie gave renditions of a few Jovi favourites. "'Bad Medicine' and 'Wanted Dead Or Alive'," wrote Suter, "lose

Sebastian Bach, Skid Row's maverick madman vocalist.

some of the Bon Jovi gloss and sound much better for the tougher approach."

He also delivered 'We All Sleep Alone' ("a real barn-burner" apparently) a Sambora/JBJ/Desmond Child composition better known as a hit for Sambora's sometime-companion Cher and 'With A Little Help From My Friends', the Beatles classic which would eventually figure on Bon Jovi's live set on their next tour—though with Jon on vocals.

Despite occasional references to a 'new age' (as in sparse, relaxing, instrumental) solo project, David

Jon swaps hairdressing tips with "Diamond" Dave Lee Roth.

> **"I DON'T WANT THE BAND TO BREAK UP. I THINK IF RICHIE LEFT THE BAND HE'D BE STUPID, BUT IF HE LEAVES, NO BIG DEAL. THE BAND WILL STILL CONTINUE...IT'S BEEN A GREAT BAND, GREAT UNIT, GOOD FRIENDS, Y'KNOW, AND IF THE TIME COMES THEN THE TIME COMES, HAVE A NICE DAY!"**
> *Jon Bon Jovi*

Bryan's own "holiday" project turned out to be a film soundtrack for a horror-movie called *The Netherworld*. "It was a cool challenge. I just said yes to the project without having a clue how to do it, but I pulled it off and it's something I'd like to explore further."

During the band lay-off, Alec John Such broke his collar bone in a motorbike accident. He admitted, "I had a problem with a muscle in my back. It looked like I might never play bass again, so I actually started having bass lessons! And, man, y'know I'm glad I did, because I've definitely improved. I feel that I'm playing better than ever."

HELPING HAND

Throughout Jon's career, he has never restricted himself to working only within the confines of the band. The solo album was just one aspect of his extramural activities—promoting the careers of other bands swallowed up what little spare time he had left. The most famous—and ultimately controversial—example of this revolved around a band put together by his old friend Dave 'Snake' Sabo, who was briefly a member of the 'Runaway'-promoting Jovi line-up.

The first time he mentioned the Skids in an interview, he said: "I'm not doing it for any financial

Paul Young, another of Jon's celebrity chums.

Jon and Diana Ross at the Grammy Awards.

Formed by Sabo and bassist/punk-rock enthusiast Rachel Bolan, Skid Row's first big break came in the recruitment of a lanky Canadian frontman called Sebastian Bach.

Bach has been described as "both beauty and the beast"—he's almost unnaturally good looking, but possessed by a raw, unpolished streak of rebellious arrogance and snotty bad-attitude, which, in the late Eighties made him perfect rock star material.

Their second piece of good luck came in the shape of almost unprecedented patronage by Jon. Aside from working as creative advisor to the band, he had them signed to Doc McGhee's management company, where they were handled by Scott McGhee, Doc's brother. Assuming all things went well they were, presumably, already on target to be the opening act for Jon's *Jersey Syndicate* world-tour, giving them the kind of launch-platform most bands could only dream of. With Jovi-related finance and guidance behind them, the band were shopped round the record labels.

GETTING OFF SKID ROW

Much to PolyGram's later regret, they passed up on Skid Row, who were eventually signed to Atlantic Records. Their self-titled debut album turned out to be a solid-if-unspectacular slice of relatively hard hitting, sharp, anthemic hard rock. It was very popular and went on to sell millions.

reward, nor am I insisting on any co-writing credits. I just wanna help a struggling group, whom I think are good, along what is a very difficult and treacherous path. I got stung by so many people when I was trying to get my first break, that anything I can do to help others will give me great pleasure."

The bit about "financial considerations" got reconsidered somewhere along the line, though, and ultimately became the cause of a serious rift between the two bands.

What really marked out Skid Row as a world-class act were their live performances—a whirlwind of flying-hair, full-on, no-nonsense guitar-riffage and Sebastian Bach's profanity-laden, spontaneous on-stage antics. Their appeal lay closer to the fierce anti-establishment rhetoric of Guns N' Roses than Bon Jovi's good-buddy, best-gang-in-town ethos and, despite their inexperience, they took to the stadium and arena stages of the *Jersey Syndicate* tour with

"Smile or I'll bite your head off"—Jon meets legendary rock madman Ozzy Osbourne.

unselfconscious ease.

Their music—rootless, generic hard rock that was neither blues-based nor coming from the ultra-heavy end of the spectrum—developed savage new teeth live and, with the heavy exposure granted to them by both the tour and MTV, the album duly took off.

At first, there was a competitive edge from which both bands could benefit. Sebastian, according to Jon, used to go into their dressing room, telling him he was gonna kick Jon's ass. "That made me work real hard when I got out there and it made me feel good when he came to the side of the stage and threw his hands up in a gesture that said I hadn't failed."

But the business side of the deal was a far from altruistic one. With perhaps a little too much commercial savvy, Jon judged that such a premium platform for the band (along with all the time he spent developing the project) was worth a hefty share of the band's publishing royalties (the money the band earn from songwriting). When the money started rolling in—and straight to the coffers of Jon's Underground organization—the Skids begged to differ.

Jon, his management and their entourage (including two of Jon's brothers) had self-styled themselves as

A real rags to riches story—Jon's Prince Charming act gave Cinderella a career boost.

"The Syndicate", a mafia-style grouping which was supposed to be an indication of the close bonds between the people working under the Bon Jovi umbrella—but perhaps Jon was taking the mafia analogy a little too far.

TOUGH TALKING

"Rock 'n' roll should be all about two people coming together as one, not getting embroiled in the business side and worrying about how to turn a $69

"HOW MANY DAYS IN YOUR LIFE DO YOU HAVE TO HEAR, 'YOU'RE ONLY THERE BECAUSE JON PUT YOU THERE'? HOW MANY TIMES CAN YOU HAVE THAT BEATEN IN YOUR HEAD? NO MATTER WHO YOU ARE, YOU'RE GONNA TURN AROUND AND SAY, 'FUCK HIM.' IT'S ONLY HUMAN NATURE."
Jon Bon Jovi

million fortune into $71 million," spat Skid Row's Sebastian Bach, who threatened never to record again until the situation was resolved.

On the second-to-last night of the *Jersey Syndicate* tour, Sebastian was drenched in ice-cold milk by Bon Jovi's road crew immediately before Skid Row were due to perform—all traditional, end-of-tour hi-jinks stuff. But Bach responded with an on-stage tirade about Jon not being man enough to hit him himself.

Jon was not amused and came looking for Bach after Skid Row's set (with, Bach insisted, just a little

"Don't shoot, I've got my hands in the air!" Young Gunner Emilio Estevez gets stuck-up.

Jon and Little Steven just jammin'.

too much back-up from his *Syndicate* buddies and bodyguards). Jon's attitude was: "If this is my house then treat it nicely, don't spit in the house, you know? That's all I would ask of anyone; if you don't like us then fine, but don't ever slag it because that's why you're here."

Punches were exchanged, but the subtext beneath the blows seemed to have more to do with the business arrangements between the bands than whether Bach had been out of order because he had, as Jon put it, "bad-mouthed me on my own stage." It was a simmering row just waiting to explode.

> **"I FOUND THE WHOLE EXPERIENCE OF DOING THE *YOUNG GUNS* SOUNDTRACK VERY REWARDING. I WROTE IT ALL MYSELF, I PRODUCED IT, AND I ALSO HAD THE CHANCE TO WORK WITH PEOPLE LIKE JEFF BECK— SOMETHING I COULD NEVER HAVE IMAGINED HAPPENING WHEN I FIRST STARTED OUT."**
> *Jon Bon Jovi*

Said to be embarrassed by the whole affair, Richie Sambora returned whatever money he had made from the Skids, and the deal was renegotiated in the Skids' favour. Deciding that he had no desire "to be a record company executive", Richie left Jon's Underground publishing and production company, which eventually mutated into Jambco Records.

TV personalities? Jon and Richie get snapped at the MTV awards.

THE FAIRY GODMOTHER

Both bands have since made reconciliatory noises. "I mean, what band comes out with their first album—I don't care who helps them—and sells four million records worldwide?" Jon noted, accepting that to have your success credited to outsider involvement

Popularity means protection: the long arm of the British law greets the guys in London.

must push a band beyond breaking point. "How many days in your life do you have to hear, 'You're only there because Jon put you there'? How many times can you have that beaten in your head? No matter who you are, you're gonna turn around and say, 'Fuck him'. It's only human nature."

Previously, Jon had helped launch the career of Cinderella, a band he first caught in a Philadelphia bar. They were, he says, phenomenal. "This guy, Tommy Kiefer, was putting out like he was playing to 1,500 seats, even though he was playing to maybe 150 people. And maybe 35 of them were paying attention to him. Everyone else was in the bar trying to get laid… He had no manager, no nothing. He wrote all the songs. And I thought, 'Wow! I gotta go do something with this guy'."

Jon handed out advice: "He had a different guitar player and a different drum player and I told him they stunk." And drew them to the attention of Derek Shulman, a senior A&R man at PolyGram. After the band had recorded their first album, he took them on tour as an opening act (making sure, of course, that Tom Kiefer was dragged back for the ritual Bon Jovi encore jam every night). And, more or less, everyone lived happily ever after.

VANITY LABELS

Cinderella enjoyed a brace of American hits with their debut album, *Night Songs*. While Cinderella

Another day, another awards ceremony for Richie, with Skid Row's Snake and friend.

Richie basking in the glow of his solo success.

never quite went on to make a *Slippery*-style leap into the super league, they managed to step out of the shadow of their mentor with the minimum of fuss and enjoy comfortable medium-ranking success. "We keep in touch, but they're definitely out on their own," reflects Jon.

The whole Skid Row experience had, perhaps, been the result of a desire to branch out and become

"MY ALBUM WAS ALL ABOUT FINDING MYSELF AGAIN. ALL THOSE YEARS OF UNRELENTING PRESSURE ON THE ROAD HAD LEFT ME BURNED OUT."
Richie Sambora

Jon looks pleased with himself, hanging out with Brigitte Nielson.

Bon Jovi salute the fans and ask them to 'Keep The Faith'.

something of a multi-media mogul. Any superstar worth their salt in the late Eighties/early Nineties was diversifying into side-projects and taking on production commitments. Prince has guided the career of a stream of (sometimes identikit) female protegees, as well as providing hit singles for acts like the Bangles and Sinead O'Connor. Madonna has cultivated, with varying degrees of success, an acting career, as well as branching out into publishing. She now has her own record label, Maverick, dedicated to cultivating new talent.

But vanity-labels and would-be talent spotting superstars are no new innovation—the Beatles had the chaotically eclectic Apple Label, the Rolling Stones released a few reggae artists on Rolling Stones Records while Led Zeppelin's Swan Song label at least enjoyed a hit with Bad Company.

Such vanity-labels are often indulgences tolerated

'Lay your autograph on me...'

> **"ALICE COOPER'S THE COOLEST. THERE YOU ARE WITH A LIVING LEGEND. I WAS MAKING HIM SING 'ONLY WOMEN BLEED' AROUND MY HOUSE. IT WAS THE BEST."**
> *Jon Bon Jovi*

ever written outside of a Bon Jovi record and, they didn't hear it the way I heard it, and didn't use it. It's called 'The Ballad Of Alice Cooper'.

"He's the coolest. There you are with a living legend. I was making him sing 'Only Women Bleed' around my house. It was the best."

One that didn't get away was 'Social Disease', which Bon Jovi recorded on their *Slippery When Wet* album—no less than Aerosmith wanted the track for an album of their own and tried to persuade the band to hand it over, with no success.

by major record labels to maintain good relations with their most important artists, but such labels rarely throw up major discoveries. Aside from the most recent Bon Jovi album, Jon's Jambco imprint has released albums by singer-songwriter Billy Falcon and Jon's old mentor, singer/multi-instrumentalist Aldo Nova—neither have made much impact.

OTHER SONGS, OTHER SINGERS

Jon's songwriting for other artists has been a little less contentious—he's written for the likes of Cher, Ted Nugent, Hall & Oates and Alice Cooper: "We wrote a song for *Trash* [Alice's 1989 album], we wrote a few for it, actually, but he only used one. We wrote 'Hell Is Living Without You', but we also wrote, in my humble opinion, the best thing I've

Just one Cornetto—Jon laps up the atmosphere.

REPAYING
THE FAITHFUL

When the band finally regrouped for what became the *Keep The Faith* album, musical climates had changed almost beyond recognition. Infamous Los Angeles rockers Guns N' Roses had enjoyed a snowballing career momentum that echoed Bon Jovi's *Slippery* break-through, but saw the band courting the kind of controversy and outrage that had been conspicuously absent from Bon Jovi's career.

Frontman Axl Rose represented the face of heavy rock in 1992. A prima donna-ish anti-hero whose eccentricities included keeping crowds waiting and taking a spiritual adviser on tour (who instructed him to avoid cities beginning with the letter "M"), Rose projected an ultimately malevolent persona.

Meanwhile, Metallica, who made their name as the brand leaders in ultra-heavy thrash metal, had recorded a self-titled break-through album, ironically, with the aid of Bon Jovi collaborator Bob Rock in the producer's chair. More accessible than previous releases, without sacrificing any of Metallica's stern heaviness, it had pushed the band to the forefront of the hard rock world, where they toured alongside Guns N' Roses, reinforcing both bands' roles as the

biggest names in metal in the Nineties.

Then there was the Nirvana factor. From the logging town of Aberdeen in America's North West, Nirvana's blend of the rough 'n' ready grunge sound of Seattle with Cheap Trick-style radio-friendly harmonies had sent them into a similar superstar orbit, and every record company in America into a panic attack as they abandoned their rock rosters to recruit new, grungier bands.

It remained pretty much business as usual for good-natured British rivals Def Leppard. But Leppard,

Jon tries to look younger, by standing next to Alice Cooper and US comedian Milton Berle

Jon at the American Music Awards, collecting another trophy for the mantlepiece.

despite a great deal of internal strife, had remained anonymous figures, their personalities virtually unknown to the rock fan in the street. As such, they were unlikely to date in the eyes of those fans. Jon Bon Jovi, on the other hand, could easily have become yesterday's man—his buoyant persona and tales of friendship seemed out of place in the harder, meaner Nineties.

OUT OF HIDING

Only the very biggest names in rock could feel remotely comfortable—most of the smaller hard rock acts had seen their record deals go to the wall and their audiences evaporate. But Jon obviously sensed that playing it safe with a by-the-numbers Bon Jovi album would be a mistake. A serious rethink was in order.

The result was *Keep The Faith*, produced by Bob Rock, who had split from Bruce Fairbairn to establish himself as a top-flight producer in his own right. Prior to recording, Jon had spent three weeks incognito, driving motorbikes round the backwoods of America—a time which was to influence the lyrical content of the album, via tracks like the 10-minute epic, 'Dry County'.

"A day when you wake up at seven in the morning

and you're out riding until seven at night is so fulfilling. Many of the places I visited I just hadn't been to before. I mean, a place like Prescott, Arizona just had nowhere Bon Jovi could play."

Jon claimed that he had "found himself" during this period. Prior to it, he explains, "I was hiding from the world. The pressure of the huge demands being placed on the band were making me go increasingly inside myself, so you always saw me surrounded by hair and great big heavy coats. I suppose they were acting like a protective shield. Since we've had all that time off I'm much happier, so I don't have to hide any more."

Symbolically, Jon returned with his trademark flowing locks drastically cropped—no more hiding behind the hair.

One bizarre rumour circulated, alleging that Jon had, in fact, burned his long locks at a barbecue and the new short crop was simply a salvaging operation. Whatever, it drew attention to the Bon Jovi 1992 style—a more serious beast than ever. While the band had dressed-down on the glitz for *New Jersey*, the old rockstar wardrobe was completely abandoned this time—not even a hint of designer-scruffiness to be seen. Plain, unfussy T-shirts and jeans were the order of the day.

STRIKE THE RIGHT BALANCE

Their new record sleeve featured the band-members' right hands touching in a three musketeers-style

Metallica, big guns of hard rock who used Bon Jovi's production guru, Bob Rock.

> **"I WAS HIDING FROM THE WORLD, SO YOU ALWAYS SAW ME SURROUNDED BY HAIR AND GREAT BIG HEAVY COATS. I SUPPOSE THEY WERE ACTING LIKE A PROTECTIVE SHIELD. SINCE WE'VE HAD ALL THAT TIME OFF I'M MUCH HAPPIER, SO I DON'T HAVE TO HIDE ANYMORE."**
> *Jon Bon Jovi*

image change from the Irish rockers—a comparison Jon "just didn't buy."

The band went so far as to have Mike Edwards of techno-pop act Jesus Jones work on dance mixes, though, after a lot of agonizing, the band decided against releasing them, feeling that they were ultimately unrepresentative.

"There are no boundaries," insisted Jon. "But I won't go off at a complete tangent just to satisfy someone else or to make this band out to be

gesture of unity. Like the rest of the *Faith* publicity material, the image was taken by Anton Cjorbin, the photographer better known for stark, black and white portraits of acts like U2 and Depeche Mode.

But new hairstyles and grainy publicity shots were only the surface—real proof came with the album's title track and first single. Based round a pumping bass line and funky drum pattern, it drew comparisons with U2's 'The Fly', another mould-breaking single which had announced a similarly bold

Still going strong, Richie looking sharp in leather.

something it's not. Let's face it, I already have a great drummer, so what do I want with a drum machine? You can't kid yourself: Bon Jovi are a rock band and with the acid-house mix I felt we were drifting into an area that was completely foreign to us, and probably to most of our audience. The secret is to strike the right balance."

"THERE ARE NO BOUNDARIES. BUT I WON'T GO OFF AT A COMPLETE TANGENT JUST TO SATISFY SOMEONE ELSE OR TO MAKE THIS BAND OUT TO BE SOMETHING IT'S NOT. LET'S FACE IT, I ALREADY HAVE A GREAT DRUMMER, SO WHAT DO I WANT WITH A DRUM MACHINE? YOU CAN'T KID YOURSELF; BON JOVI ARE A ROCK BAND."
Jon Bon Jovi

Jon later conceded that, perhaps, the band could have stretched themselves a little further on the record. But he has always been cautious about heading too far off the beaten path—early on, he was namechecking Elton John and Tom Petty as influences

Giving till it hurts.

Alec shows off his lurid new bass guitar.

at an age when most of his contemporaries couldn't see beyond AC/DC and Aerosmith; something which the band's songwriting hinted at. But, while Jon was one of the first American rock stars to acknowledge U2 as a "rock", rather than "alternative" band, his appreciation of Bono and Co would have been hard to detect on record, up until *Keep The Faith*'s title track.

Likewise, a much mooted collaboration with Prince never seemed to get past the talking about it stage.

THE NEW DIRECTION

Keep The Faith was "the biggest leap we've made between records since *7800° Fahrenheit* and *Slippery*", observes Richie Sambora, adding: "But we didn't want to leave behind the 30 million people that bought the last two Bon Jovi albums. So we didn't want to make a Pink Floyd record—but we needed to evolve our own style."

Slightly more radical intentions had originally been planned for the release. While still making videos for the *New Jersey* album, Jon had told one reporter: "I would like to make our *Sergeant Pepper* next time— that's the ultimate goal, and maybe by the next album we'll be there."

In the end, *Keep The Faith* breathed just enough new life into the old Bon Jovi sound, reshaping it in places, but cautiously keeping the old fans happy with up-beat popsters like 'Sleep When I'm Dead'. Although the title track featured more than a hint of a groove, tracks like the mammoth, moody 'Dry County' and the lush ballad, 'Bed Of Roses', made it clear that the real direction was an expansion of the maturity which *New Jersey* had heralded.

"Because my confidence was so high after doing a solo album, I wrote the bulk of the new record myself." says Jon. "This time we didn't feel as though we had to keep up with anything in my past. We'd all been through the mill and came back feeling better

No frill, no fuss and—biggest shock of all—no long hair!

"KEEP THE FAITH WAS THE BIGGEST LEAP WE'VE MADE BETWEEN RECORDS SINCE 7800° FAHRENEHIT AND SLIPPERY... BUT WE DIDN'T WANT TO LEAVE BEHIND THE 30 MILLION PEOPLE THAT BOUGHT THE LAST TWO BON JOVI ALBUMS. SO WE DIDN'T WANT TO MAKE A PINK FLOYD RECORD—BUT WE NEEDED TO EVOLVE OUR OWN STYLE."
Richie Sambora

ARE THEY BACK, OR NOT?

When Jon entered the publicity fray to introduce the world to his new album, he was a tired figure on a fairly short fuse—the press, after all, had stirred up serious mischief with their allegations of a split in the ranks. The intrusions of the press, however, is something he's always tolerated as coming with the turf—unlike stars who shun the media like, say, Prince or Axl Rose.

"The fans that are so loyal to the band deserve to know what's going on. Not what the journalist has to make up because he can't get an interview. So I'd

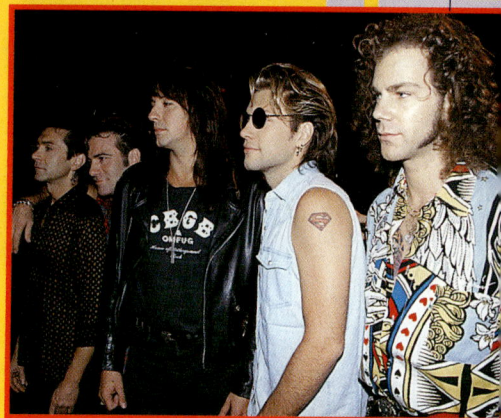

After the break: reunited, and ready to rock.

for it. Songs like 'Bed Of Roses' and 'Dry County' mean a lot to me because they came out of experiences I'd had since we made the last record. I couldn't have written those songs five years ago.

"If you just stay the same you become a parody of yourself. I couldn't imagine me in the white Elvis suit singing 'Living On A Prayer', y'know?"

Wild at heart, the new-look Jon models a stylish new snake-skin jacket.

rather call you and tell you first hand," he told one reporter. The teen-pop end of the media, though, is something dealt with through gritted teeth.

"They ask really dumb questions and nothing pertaining to music. You get asked ten questions in a row like that, when you've just flown from Australia to Portugal which took 27 hours… oh shit, I don't need that right now."

But this time around, the questions on every reporter's lips were less trivial than the colour of Jon's socks or the band's favourite foods: had the band split for real, and were they only back together for financial reasons?

"I wondered in my heart if there would be a Bon Jovi to go back to," admits Jon. "But deep in my heart I knew there was a magic in what the band did together. We'd have been complete assholes to ignore the God-given phenomenon we'd been gifted with. We broke up because our last album only sold ten million copies? What sort of assholes would that make us?!"

For the magic to work, however, some old ties had to be severed. Jon decided to split from long-time manager 'Doc' McGhee a decision which Richie (apparently reluctantly) went along with.

"In order for us not to slip into our old habits it was better just to turn the page," explained Jon. In fact it's Jon who now more or less manages the

The restyled, modern look of Jon Bon Jovi—a force to be reckoned with into the Nineties.

entire Bon Jovi operation himself.

In a show of unity, Jon roped in some of the band's more low-key members for promotional duties and only group shots were allowed in early *Keep The Faith* photo shoots—no solo shots of Jon.

"I was the mystery guy," admitted Alec John Such, who was, indeed, the band's biggest unknown quantity. "I always seemed to be in the background in the past, cos that's just how it was when we put the band together. I could dig it, cos it meant that I didn't get hassled so much, or do as much work. Hey, I was lazy! But now I feel that I do want to contribute more."

"Al's liked his anonymity," confirms Jon, "but trying to get him to do anything in the past was like pulling teeth."

PLAYING THE BAR

The band played a number of low-key gigs to tie in with the album's launch, including a show at the Fast Lane in New Jersey—billed, like the old days, as Jon Bongiovi And The Wild Ones—and one at London's Astoria Theatre.

Instead of the triumphant entrance of old, in London he simply strolled on-stage with the minimum of fuss and none of his usual crowd-stirring antics. Leading the band through 'A Little Help From My Friends', the old Beatles/Joe Cocker standard, he sealed the reunion in a style that was at once both classy and relaxed.

The emphasis was placed firmly on the idea of Bon Jovi as a solid, knock-out live band—naturalistic, well-crafted, loose enough to slip into the well-worn

> **"BECAUSE MY CONFIDENCE WAS SO HIGH AFTER DOING A SOLO ALBUM, I WROTE THE BULK OF THE NEW RECORD MYSELF. THIS TIME WE DIDN'T FEEL AS THOUGH WE HAD TO KEEP UP WITH ANYTHING IN MY PAST. WE'D ALL BEEN THROUGH THE MILL AND CAME BACK FEELING BETTER FOR IT. SONGS LIKE 'BED OF ROSES' AND 'DRY COUNTRY' I COULDN'T HAVE WRITTEN FIVE YEARS AGO."**
> *Jon Bon Jovi*

After his bluesy solo album, Richie steps back into the Bon Jovi spotlight.

shoes of the the old classics. Peggy Lee's 'Fever' and the Animals' rousing 'We've Got To Get Out Of This Place' both made a set appearance, as Jon the rockstar took a backseat to Bon Jovi the bar band.

Of course, that's not to say that Jon neglected the hits. As well as old favourites like 'You Give Love A Bad Name' and 'Born To Be My Baby', the band seamlessly added Jon's solo smash 'Blaze of Glory' to their repertoire.

In previous years (Moscow Peace Festival aside) Jon had fought shy of any sort of political affiliation. But the recent election of Bill Clinton as American President caused him to comment, at London's Astoria, that former President Bush "done fucked up" by forgetting that "the kids of today are the presidents of tomorrow," drawing unspoken parallels between his band's rebirth and implying that Bon Jovi shared Clinton's grass roots "time for change" vibe. He followed through with an acoustic version of 'Living On A Prayer' that washed away the showbiz panache, revealing a more serious side to the song.

Alec raises his bass to salute the crowd.

A NOD TO GRUNGE

"Bon Jovi: Killed By Grunge?" asked one English rock magazine when news filtered through that US sales for *Keep The Faith* were comparatively sluggish. Jon maintained a dignified response, talking in terms of

Remember this? Fresh-faced Jon in hairier days.

personal satisfaction, career longevity and, of course, the fact that five million sales world wide (since increased to six) was still nothing to be sniffed at.

Asked whether he felt threatened by the influx of grunge bands, instead of going on the defensive, he wisely opted to acknowledge their contribution to the rock scene.

"Those guys are talking from their guts, and there's a big difference between this style of music and some

> **"I WONDERED IN MY HEART IF THERE WOULD BE A BON JOVI TO GO BACK TO. BUT DEEP IN MY HEART I KNEW THERE WAS A MAGIC IN WHAT THE BAND DID TOGETHER. WE'D HAVE BEEN COMPLETE ASSHOLES TO IGNORE THE GOD-GIVEN PHENOMENON WE'D BEEN GIFTED WITH."**
> *Jon Bon Jovi*

of the crotch-rock and syrupy love songs that heavy rock was identifying itself with a few years ago."

Singling out Eddie Vedder of Pearl Jam for praise, he claimed to share many similar influences with the Seattle bands—Kiss, Cheap Trick, Seventies rock 'n' roll bands. But some differences too: "These days kids are a little more pissed off with living in a world that's not the greatest place. For myself, I know it's a

Jon faces up to the future.

pissy place, but why should I write about the obvious when I've been so lucky in my life? Being an optimist, I prefer to write something positive instead."

Even if *Keep The Faith*'s sales were solid rather than spectacular, the appetite for the Bon Jovi in concert experience remained as great as ever. In Europe the band managed, if anything, to increase their popularity as a live act—having played England's Milton Keynes Bowl once on the *New Jersey* tour, they managed to fill it two nights running in September 1993.

Happily married to childhood sweetheart Dorothea, with a baby daughter in Stephanie Rose Bongiovi (despite stories that he'd call his first-born Elvis, regardless of gender), Jon Bon Jovi in his early 30s is maturing nicely from the late-teens prodigy who hussled his way round the New Jersey club circuit. He's avoided self-parody and, in years to come, will undoubtedly become one of rock's venerable elder statesmen. And, of course, he can still cut it live.

"It's not my worry that Axl Rose is selling more tickets than I am," he said in the Summer of 1993. "God bless him. You know what I mean? Have a nice time, pal. I've done it. I'm not worried about keeping up with the Joneses. All I have to know is, when I go out there at night, did these people think I kicked their asses? Great. That's what matters."

discOgraphy

BON JOVI ALBUMS

BON JOVI (1984)
7800° FAHRENHEIT (1985)
SLIPPERY WHEN WET (1986)
NEW JERSEY (1988)
KEEP THE FAITH (1992)

JON BON JOVI SOLO ALBUMS

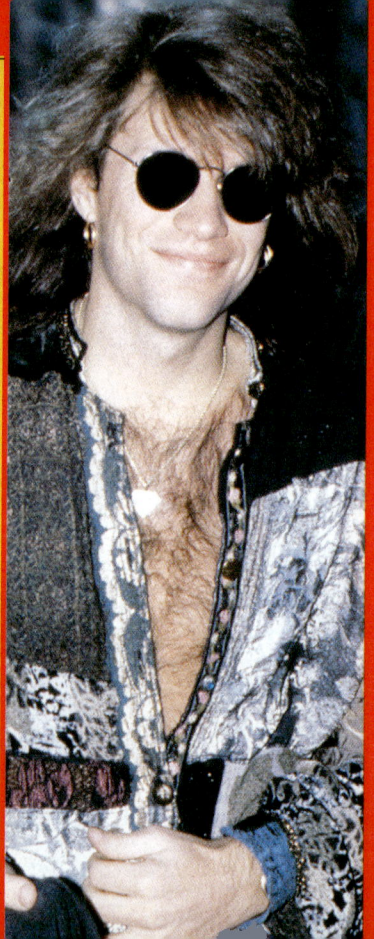

'Blaze Of Glory': Songs Written and Performed By Jon Bon Jovi, Inspired by *The Film Young Guns II*. (1990).

RICHIE SAMBORA SOLO ALBUMS

RICHIE SAMBORA: Stranger In This Town (1991)

SINGLES

Runaway
In And Out Of Love
Hardest Part Is The Night
You Give Love A Bad Name
Living On A Prayer
Never Say Goodbye
Bad Medicine
Born To Be My Baby
I'll Be There For You
Lay Your Hands On Me
Living In Sin
Keep The Faith
Bed Of Roses
In These Arms
I'll Sleep When I'm Dead
I Believe

Chronology

1. 2 March 1962 birth of John Francis Bongiovi
2. July 1983 signed with PolyGram records
3. 1984 release of first album *Bon Jovi*
4. 1985 3rd at Monsters of Rock festival Castle Donington (England)
5. 1985 release of *7800° Fahrenheit*
6. 1986 release of *Slippery When Wet*
7. 1988 release of *New Jersey*
8. 1988 Headlined at Monsters of Rock festival Castle Donington
9. 1 November 1988 first night of *New Jersey* world tour (England)
10. August 1989 Moscow's Olympic Stadium
11. 1990 Jon Bon Jovi releases solo album *Blaze of Glory*
12. July 1990 rumours of split
13. 1991 Richie Sambora releases solo album *Stranger In This Town*
14. 1992 release of *Keep The Faith*
15. September 1993 Milton Keynes *Keep The Faith* tour

Picture Acknowledgements

Photographs reproduced by kind permission of **London Features International**; **Pictorial Press**/Todd Kaplan,/Bob Gruen,/Bob Scott,/Dominick Conde,/Vinnie Zuffante,/Robin Kaplan.

Front cover picture: Retna Pictures/Michael Malfer

index

A

AC/DC 101
Aerosmith 37,101
Alice Cooper 37
Albums:
    7800° Fahrenheit 26
    Blaze of Glory 69
    Bon Jovi 22
    Keep The Faith 96
    Slippery When Wet 36
    New Jersey 44
Atlantic records 80
Avasec, Marc 22

B

Bacon, Kevin 25
Beck, Jeff 71
Black Sabbath 62
Bongiovi, Carol 10

Bongiovi, Tony 15
Bongiovi, John Francis 10
Bongiovi, John, Sr 10
Bryan, David 9
Bush, George 109

C

Castle Donington 39
Child, Desmond 37
Cinderella 88
Cjorbin, Anton 99
Clinton, Bill 109
Cocker, Joe 106

D

Def Leppard 9
Depeche Mode 99
Dickinson, Bruce 42
Dominion, London 35

Dublin 7
Dukes, The 12
Duran Duran 26

E

Elliot, Joe 9

F

Footloose 25
Fairbairn, Bruce 36
Ford, Lita 57, 60

G

Gorky Park 62
Guns N' Roses 81, 96

H

Hammersmith Odeon 35

I

Iron Maiden 42

J

Jesus Jones 99
Joel, Billy 63
John, Elton 63

K

Kerrang magazine 23

Kiss 25

L

Larson, Lance 13
Led Zeppelin 9
Lee, Tommy 65
Little Steven 26
Lofgren, Nils 26

M

Madison Square Garden 22
McGhee, Doc 57
Metallica 96
Moscow Peace Festival 61
Motley Crüe 23

N

New Jersey world tour 7
Nirvana 96

O

Osbourne, Ozzy 62

P

Pearl Jam 111
Perry, Joe 60
PolyGram 20
Prince 101

Q

Quiet Riot 23

R

Rashbaum, David 10
Ratt 32
Relationships 28
Rock, Bob 36
Rose, Axl 96

S

Sabo, Dave 18
Sambora, Richie 9
Sambora solo career 73
Scorpions 25
Sixx, Nikki 62
Skid Row 18,62
Smuggling 61
Snider, Dee 42
Songs:
    Bad Medicine 53
    Bed Of Roses 103
    Born To Be My Baby 53
    Hardest Part Is The Night ..28
    I'll Sleep When I'm Dead . 103
    Keep The Faith 101
    Lay Your Hands On Me 53
    Living On A Prayer 37
    Runaway..........................17
    You Give Love
        A Bad Name................37
Spectrum, The (Philadelphia) 13
Springsteen, Bruce 11
Squire, Billy 16
Stanley, Paul 42
Stewart, Rod 25
Such, Alec John 18

T

Torres, Tico 9
Twisted Sister 17
Tyler, Steven 25

U

U2....................................99, 101

V

Van Halen, Eddie 18
Vedder, Eddie 111

W

Wild Ones 11

Y

Young, Neil 26